C000056281

The Buccaneer at Eastbourne, East Sussex – brick, stucco and marble; 'Jacobethan' towers; 'Oriental' domes; sash, Venetian and 'Wrenaissance' windows – an epitome of the buccaneering eclecticism of public-house architecture at the zenith of its exuberance.

The Victorian Public House

Richard Tames

A Shire book

'When you have lost your inns, drown your empty selves, for you will have lost the last of England.'
Hilaire Belloc

ACKNOWLEDGEMENTS
Photographs are acknowledged as follows: Michael Bass, page 16; Cadbury Lamb, pages 1, 3, 4 (top), 13 (top), 19 (both), 23, 24 (bottom), 29 (top), 36 (bottom), 37 (top), 39, 40, and front cover; Richard Tames, page 4 (bottom), 7, 9, 11 (both), 12 (both), 13 (bottom), 14 (bottom), 15 (top), 18 (top), 21, 22, 24 (top), 25 (all), 26, 27, 30 (both), 31 (all), 32 (both), 33 (bottom), 35 (bottom), 36 (top two) and 38.

Cover: *The Sherlock Holmes, just south of Trafalgar Square, London, was until 1957 the Northumberland Arms, taking its name from Northumberland House, demolished in 1874, or Northumberland Avenue, laid out that same year. (It was while staying at the Northumberland Hotel, then opposite, that Sir Henry Baskerville lost his shoe in Sir Arthur Conan Doyle's celebrated Sherlock Holmes adventure of 1902, 'The Hound of the Baskervilles'.)*

British Library Cataloguing in Publication Data: Tames, Richard. The Victorian public house. – (Shire album; 423) 1. Bars (Drinking establishments) – Great Britain – History – 19th century 2. Drinking behaviour – Great Britain – History – 19th century 3. Brewing industry – Great Britain – History – 19th century 4. Working class – Great Britain – Social life and customs – 19th century I. Title 647.9'541'09034 ISBN 0 7478 0573 3.

Published in 2003 by Shire Publications Ltd, Cromwell House, Church Street, Princes Risborough, Buckinghamshire HP27 9AA, UK. (Website: www.shirebooks.co.uk)
Copyright © 2003 by Richard Tames. First published 2003. Shire Album 423. ISBN 0 7478 0573 3.
Richard Tames is hereby identified as the author of this work in accordance with Section 77 of the Copyright, Designs and Patents Act 1988.

Printed in Great Britain by CIT Printing Services Ltd, Press Buildings, Merlins Bridge, Haverfordwest, Pembrokeshire SA61 1XF.

CONTENTS

Burton upon Trent's original Leopard Inn was built in the early nineteenth century. Acquired by Charrington's of Stepney in 1872, it was reconstructed in the 'London style'. Note the proprietorial inscription on the entablature and proclamation of the availability of 'London Stout".

INN, TAVERN AND ALEHOUSE

The earliest inns, austere dormitories founded by monasteries for pilgrims, were soon rivalled by commercial establishments providing food and drink as well as lodging. From 1393 onwards

inns had to display an identifying sign. This was a tradition passed down from Roman times, when *tabernae* (inns) used to hang out a garland of vine leaves to show that they had wine. With the contraction of viticulture in post-Roman Britain, a small evergreen shrub was often substituted. Early alehouses imitated the custom by hanging out ale stakes, used to stir the brew. The form of the sign ordered by the 1393 act was not specified, but the cheapest type used was a bit of wood – hence 'The Crooked Billet'. The

Left: *Built in 1828, the Bush in Cockermouth, Cumbria, has a sign that echoes the garlands hung out by Roman 'tabernae'.*

Below: *The Anchor at Wadesmill, Hertfordshire, a listed building, was clearly once two separate properties, the Victorian part being to the left. Located by a bridge at the bottom of a steep hill, it was once an important stop for changing stagecoach teams on the Great North Road. England's first turnpike gate was set up at Wadesmill in 1663. Nearby Ware was from the fifteenth century until 1994 a premier centre for malting and a crucial supplier to London brewers via the river Lea.*

For medieval housewives brewing ale was a daily task, commemorated in the surname Brewster (as opposed to the masculine Brewer). Made without hops, ale spoiled quickly. Skilled brewsters indicated a surplus for sale by putting out a broom as a makeshift sign.

1552 Licensing Act gave magistrates control of licensed premises. From the 1660s regular coaching services expanded demand for resting-places, refreshment and relays of horses, creating employment for ostlers, grooms, cooks, scullions, waiters and boot-boys. Inns were also used for auctions, inquests and meetings of local vestrymen, churchwardens and magistrates. Soldiers were regularly lodged in licensed premises, barracks being rare until Victoria's reign.

Inns were forbidden to serve local residents but were open for travellers at any hour (just who constituted a *bona fide* traveller was perennially contentious). Taverns, regulated by different licensing arrangements, provided food and drink but were forbidden to shelter guests, and kept limited hours. Taverns, essentially urban

A stagecoach passing through Witham, Essex, en route to the port of Harwich, c.1830. Within two decades the Eastern Counties Railway would drive this coaching trade out of existence. Notice the three inn signs to the left of the coach.

establishments, in the eighteenth century served as rendezvous for business and conversation among merchants, ministers, poets and wits. A century later, such men had deserted them for the exchange and the gentlemen's club. Statistician G. R. Porter noted in 1852 that 'no person above the rank of labouring man or artisan would venture to go into a public house' – except perhaps for self-consciously rebellious Bohemian artists, writers and show-business hangers-on. Middle-class desertion left the tavern to metamorphose into 'the pub' as a prime bastion of Victorian working-class culture.

The alehouse or beerhouse was literally what its name proclaimed, a place that sold only beer (which was then safer to drink than water). Consisting usually of 'kitchen' and 'tap room' and furnished with simple benches and tables, it normally had neither bar nor cellar, serving straight from casks ranked against the wall; but it was a welcome refuge for tramps and beggars in funds, navvies, seasonal harvesters, migrant workers, street vendors, stall-holders, off-duty servants and lodgers trapped in even worse domestic settings. Larger establishments might have a 'parlour', with chairs and pictures, for more discriminating customers.

During Victoria's reign, beerhouses typically became larger, the kitchen and tap room being replaced by the saloon (from the French *salon*, implying a room of impressive size for social functions) and public bar, a counter replacing the serving hatch. A distinctive northern configuration emerged – a narrow corridor giving access to various small rooms. Southern configurations featured an entrance to an off-sales point, flanked by saloon and public bars.

A drayman delivers beer in a crowded Victorian Street. Cellar storage was preferable for keeping beer at an appropriate temperature.

In beerhouses with cellars the primitive ranking of casks was replaced by basement storage, the beer being drawn up by newly invented hydraulic beer-engines. By the 1840s beerhouses were offering sandwiches, bread, cheese and pickles. Fried fish was sold with bread, not chips. Street pie-sellers were encouraged in. Workmen often brought in their midday meal of chops, offal or sausages to be cooked, paying a charge for this service, condiments and cutlery.

In the industrial Midlands and the North, the public bar was often called 'the vault'. At Ilkeston in Derbyshire this pub commemorates Captain Gregory, a local philanthropist. Note the attempt at architectural presence despite an awkwardly irregular site – symmetrical rounded arches surmounted by a gable with finial.

BEER AND BREWERIES

Meux's Brewery, London – the site is now occupied by the Dominion Theatre on Tottenham Court Road. Breweries were one of London's few large-scale capital-intensive industries. Whitbread's Chiswell Street brewery pioneered the use of steam technology in London brewing.

In 1801 home brewing accounted for half of total British beer consumption. A century later the figure was virtually nil. Home brewing, like home baking, required space and time but urbanisation restricted living space as industrialisation lengthened working hours.

In 1816 there were 48,000 licensed alehouses in England and Wales, of which 14,200 belonged to breweries, 10,800 to occupiers and 22,700 to third-party investors. Between 1830 and 1881 the number of public houses in England and Wales rose by more than half. By 1900 there were 100,000 on-licences operative in England and Wales, 90 per cent of which were owned by breweries. There were also 12,000 off-licences, an urban innovation first established in 1834 in response to the advent of cheaper bottled beers.

Annual *per capita* beer consumption in 1800 was 33 gallons (150 litres), falling markedly to 19 gallons (86 litres) in the 'Hungry Forties', then peaking at 34 gallons (155 litres) in 1876, before tapering off to 27 gallons (123 litres) by 1914. Excise-duty increases doubled the price of gin to 6d a quartern (quarter pint) between 1830 and 1900, while beer remained remarkably stable at around 4d a quart. The drink trade struggled to maintain sales against pressure from the temperance movement, shifts in excise duty and growing competition from tea, coffee, cocoa, soft drinks and clean water. (Watering beer, incidentally, was not made illegal until 1885.) As competition for market share intensified in the last quarter of the

nineteenth century, brewers and their tenants made huge investments in premises, fittings and facilities, drawing on new sources of capital. Guinness became a public company in 1886, Bass in 1888, Whitbread in 1889, Watney, Combe & Reid in 1898. Between 1886 and 1899 brewery flotations raised a staggering £185,000,000. The brewers also widened their range of attractions, as social investigator Charles Booth shrewdly noted in 1888: 'the licensed victuallers begin to see that they cannot live by drink alone'. To understand how they ever thought they could, one must go back a lifetime.

McMullen's brewery in Hertford combines an exuberant fusion of architectural motifs. The overall effect is less industrial than of a Victorian spa complex surmounted by an oriental fortress. Originally the Hope brewery, the site was taken over by McMullen's in 1890. Hertford also had at least three other breweries and was historically a major centre of the malting industry.

THE GIN PALACE

The 1825 Budget's reduction of duty on spirits by almost half doubled legal consumption immediately. A new kind of drinking establishment emerged in London to meet this surge in demand. Capitalising on improvements in sheet-glass manufacture, the gin palace's design featured large windows and introduced the bar counter to produce a revolutionary layout based on the model of the single-storey shop rather than the old-style tavern, with its parlour, 'coffee-room', 'snugs' and upstairs private rooms for meetings or dining. Host and guest became retailer and customer. Thompson & Fearon's on Holborn Hill, designed by John Buonarotti Papworth (1775–1847), set a style rapidly imitated in response to the proliferation of 31,000 new beerhouses as a result of the 1830 Beer Act. This legislation, coupled with the total abolition of duty on beer (though not malt), cutting its price by a fifth, aimed to promote the consumption of beer rather than gin and made it possible for anyone to open a beerhouse on the purchase of a 2 guinea licence (3 guineas from 1834). At 3d a quartern, however, gin remained competitive with beer.

Gas lighting, another technological novelty, took until the 1850s to penetrate even middle-class homes. Gin-palace design was therefore striking in the 1830s for featuring both external and internal gas lighting. Large mirrors increased the level of illumination and, strategically placed, improved staff surveillance of the often wayward clientele.

The prolific illustrator George Cruikshank depicted gin-shop customers encircled by a giant mantrap while nightwatchman Death summons them to their inevitable destiny.

Massive external lanterns, copied from the gin-shop model, became a common feature of the urban public house and were frequently placed at corner sites, where their brightness could penetrate the gloom of converging streets. Superfluous external lanterns remain a feature of many modern public houses designed in a pastiche of the Victorian mode.

Charles Dickens observed wonderingly that the increasing popularity of the gin palace was 'depositing splendid mansions, stone balustrades, rosewood fittings, immense lamps and illuminated clocks at the corner of every street'. But there was minimal comfort inside to discourage lingering. There were no snugs for convivial drinking groups. No food was served. Many had

Ornate glass windows and woodwork at the Prince Alfred, Maida Vale, London. The interior still features screens subdividing the drinking area and a fine patterned plaster ceiling.

Above and right: *The Ladbroke Arms, discreetly tucked away in a London side-street, was intended for the refreshment of servants employed in the massive terrace houses of the surrounding Ladbroke estate as it was developed from the 1840s onwards. Note the large reproduction of a photograph of the pub c.1900 on the outside wall. This reveals that the smart blue house to the rear was formerly a stable. Note also the removal of the advertising balustrades.*

no seats. Naturally, pastimes such as dominoes or bagatelle, which interfered with non-stop inebriation, were conspicuous by their absence. The *Building News* commented sourly in 1857 that gin palaces were 'large buildings of splendid elevation fitted up in a style of grandeur ... quite unsuited to the rational demands of the humbler classes that throng them daily ... the corner public is radiant of gas, redolent of mahogany and glittering in mirrors, there are no settles, no stools.... At the bar the dropper in to drink must stand ... and move on when tired.' And so they did. One contemporary journalist, observing a Holborn gin palace, estimated that in a single hour an average of six people entered every minute.

While gin palaces proliferated promiscuously in the slums, in purpose-built suburbs pubs were controlled. Developer Thomas

The Ambrose Hotel, Barrow-in-Furness, Cumbria, of 1861 has readopted a bold Victorian livery but the former side entrances, originally built to speed up access for casual drinkers, remain blocked off.

Cubitt prided himself on allowing one pub to every 160 houses 'so that the Publicans may have sufficient trade to keep their houses in respectable order'. In swanky Belgravia he confined pubs to mews sites. In less prestigious Pimlico he allowed them on main streets but not on squares. Such scrupulous development was the exception rather than the rule. Most rapidly growing suburbs were characterised by a general free-for-all mentality among small-scale speculative builders, resulting in the construction of licensed premises every two hundred paces or so. Public houses became quite literally cornerstones of urban development. By putting up a pub and becoming its first licensee, the builder acquired a site office as well as a works canteen, recycling his wage bill back into his own pocket. The business was then sold on to finance further development.

This Pimlico pub was rebuilt in 1846 on the site of the former Orange Tree Coffee House and Tavern, dating from 1776. Its micro-brewery dates from around 1979.

Station hotels, larger than the greatest coaching inn, brought a new sophistication and efficiency to catering for travellers. In provincial cities lacking restaurants they also provided the best venue for public functions, but not all succeeded. This imposing pile, opened by millionaire railway contractor Sir Samuel Morton Peto at Colchester, Essex, in 1843, soon proved unsuccessful and was converted into a lunatic asylum.

RAILWAY REVOLUTIONS

The railways inevitably killed off coaching inns. A London travel guide of 1871 asserted that they had 'become comfortable middle-class hotels', ironically 'with railway booking-offices attached'. Reminiscing in 1906, Colchester landlord Joseph Phillips listed former inns that had been changed variously to a saddler's, 'a select club house', warehouses, a fried-fish shop and even a temperance hotel. Phillips identified factors other than the railway that were fatal to the coaching inn, notably the abolition of open hustings for voting at elections and the consequent end of 'treating' potential voters and, peculiar to garrison towns, the discontinuance of paying army pensions to veterans in pubs and of billeting militia there during training.

Along with other existing hostelries in Berkhamsted, Hertfordshire, the Goat, dating from c.1782, was rebuilt rather than closed in the nineteenth century. Their prosperity might have foundered as the previously important stagecoach trade collapsed but for the compensating stimulus of the Grand Junction Canal (1798) and the railway (1837) and the associated industries they sustained.

14

'Crocker's Folly' – originally the Crown – in Aberdeen Place, St John's Wood, London, was commissioned in 1898 from Charles H. Worley, who gave it an interior hailed by the 'Licensed Victuallers' Gazette' as more like 'the hall of some magnificent modern mansion ... than the saloon of a tavern'. Erected on the assumption that it would stand opposite the terminus of the last railway line to be built into central London, it was blighted by the railway company's decision to press on a mile further to Marylebone. The luckless proprietor jumped to his death from an upper window – hence the name.

Before the emergence of the railways a two-day journey by horse and cart represented a brewery's effective radius of distribution. The railways made possible national distribution of beers brewed in Burton upon Trent, where the calcium sulphate (gypsum) in the soil enabled brewers to produce light, sparkling ales, strongly contrasting with London breweries' dark porter. The abolition of

The Great White Horse Hotel, Ipswich, Suffolk, was a former coaching inn but, located in an expanding port, was able to reinvent itself as an hotel. Note the separate bar entrance at the extreme left past the third window from the main entrance.

15

The Britannia in Tring, Hertfordshire, was built in the late 1830s for the benefit of men working on the London to Birmingham railway. This postcard was published c.1910 – note the telegraph poles but also the absence of motor traffic. Note also the welcome notice to cyclists. The Britannia became a private house in 1980.

glass duty in 1847, greatly cheapening drinking vessels, put a premium on clear pale ales, as opposed to their murkier counterparts. By 1881, 8000 of Burton's 39,000 population were employed in the borough's thirty or so breweries. Some, including Bass, Marston's and Allsopp's, originated locally. Others, such as Charrington, Mann, Crossman & Paulin and Truman, Hanbury & Buxton, were branches of London firms.

In the 1860s, drinkers in Newcastle upon Tyne had only sweet, dark mild, based on poor-quality local water; pale ales from Burton or Scotland almost completely supplanted this by the 1890s. Tyneside then accounted for a third of William Younger of Edinburgh's entire output and a quarter of the production of Scotland's six leading brewers. Local breweries fought back by amalgamating to create Newcastle Breweries Limited and North Eastern Breweries. Consolidation became the order of the day as brewing firms closed down small operations and further enlarged big ones. In 1870 there were 26,506 breweries producing fewer than a thousand barrels a year; by 1914 nine-tenths of these had gone. Between 1890 and 1900 alone the number of operative brewing plants (not firms) fell from 11,322 to 6460 while output rose by 20 per cent.

An incidental by-product of the railways was the island bar, invented by Isambard Kingdom Brunel, engineer of the Great Western Railway. Challenged with only ten minutes to serve train-loads of passengers decanted on to Swindon station, Brunel decided that a circular counter was best for optimum access. Experience outside the railways confirmed that an 'island' configuration offered excellent overall supervision of drinkers, although glass 'snob screens', diminishing eye-contact with staff, could be inserted for privacy.

16

REGULATING DRINK AND DRINKERS

The 1839 Metropolitan Police Act allowed prohibition of Sunday morning opening in the capital, the first statutory regulation of opening hours. This became general practice throughout England by 1848. Scotland followed suit in 1853, Ireland in 1878 and Wales in 1881. As Peter Haydon has noted, limits on Sunday drinking were often ignored – but ignored prudently. Blatant defiance brought retribution.

The 1839 Act additionally banned those under the age of sixteen from drinking on licensed premises in London but this did not become general practice until 1872, and selling liquor to those under fourteen was banned only in 1901.

Also introduced by the 1839 Act was a 40 shilling fine for drunkenness in London – two weeks' wages for a working man, against the national norm of 5 shillings. An 1872 Act rationalised fines on a sliding scale, ranging from 10 shillings for a first offence to

CAUTION.

Whereas, it is understood that the Practice of

SELLING BEER

IN PRIVATE HOUSES,

Without a Licence, prevails to a considerable extent in this neighbourhood.

Now, I GIVE NOTICE and WARNING, that if the Occupier of any House erected on the Property of the late EDMUND WILLIAMS, Esq., of Maesruddud, be detected in the above illegal Practice, he will not only be proceeded against for the Penalty, but measures will be taken to forfeit the Lease under which the Premises may be held.

Dated this 8th October, 1851,

A. WADDINGTON,

SOLICITOR TO THE ESTATE.

H. HUGHES, PRINTER, BOOKBINDER, AND STATIONER, PONTYPOOL.

Backdoor business – a Welsh landlord warns tenants of the risk they run selling beer from unlicensed private premises.

The Fox and Hounds, Passmore Street, London, of c.1860 was initially granted a licence to sell only beer because the estate landlord, the future Duke of Westminster, was a temperance campaigner strongly opposed to spirits.

40 shillings for the third. In 1879 Dr Cameron's Habitual Drunkards' Act established retreats to treat addiction. Patients had to pay for themselves and remained until pronounced cured. In 1898 magistrates were empowered to commit criminal inebriates to reformatories.

Heavy fines for public drunkenness did less to deter it than did the advent of uniformed police from 1829 onwards. In 1857 some 75,000 drunk and drunk-and-disorderly cases were brought; by 1876 the number had risen above 200,000 to account for over 40 per cent of non-indictable offences brought before magistrates. Variations in local zeal and licensing policy may account for Manchester being apparently five, and Liverpool ten, times as drunken a place as Birmingham. Police exercised wide discretion. Gentlemanly drunks and respectable working men were usually ignored or even helped to a cab. The poorest and shabbiest were invariably the most often charged.

Pubs produced other evils than inebriation. Much impoverishment was caused by the paying of wages in pubs (common among outdoor workers, for example building labourers or dockers) or, as in the Potteries, by the paying of teams of workers in large notes, requiring a publican to make change – and pass a percentage back to the foreman with whom he was colluding. Potter Charles Shaw remembered how 'Boys and women would be pressed to drink .... Meantime the publican kept the change back ... until he saw his adult customers ... settled for a night's booze... towards ten o'clock, poor wretched women would appear and entreat their husbands to go home'. In the 1870s Black Country miners were still being bribed into illegal overtime by forepayment of beer awaiting them at a designated pub. The paying of wages on licensed premises was finally banned in 1883.

The 1869 Wine and Beerhouse Act, ending the 'Free Trade in Beer' prevailing since 1830,

Police enjoyed a wide measure of discretion in dealing with drunks, as illustrated in this cartoon of 1902.

The New Navigation is at Birchill, Walsall, West Midlands. Canals, originally known as 'navigations', were dug by navigators, hence 'navvies', whose high earnings and rough lifestyle ensured that most of their weekly wage was rapidly recycled in lock-side hostelries erected to serve these new arteries of commerce and communication.

transferred beerhouse licences from the excise office to magistrates, who could henceforth control sales of beer and wine as they did spirits. As anticipated, this reduced the number of licences, increased their value and encouraged the growth of tied houses as brewers mobilised capital for investment in larger, more lavish premises. An 1872 Act brought all drink retailers under licensing magistrates, who could refuse to renew the licences of publicans permitting gambling or prostitution or serving drunks or uniformed police. Magistrates could also reduce outlets by offering brewers a new licence only in return for two or more old ones. Another limiting factor was the increasing cost of licences, based on rates, which, after 1869, were revalued every five years. In 1882 magistrates gained control of off-licences, and in 1891 the landmark case of *Sharp v. Wakefield* determined that Justices of the Peace could refuse licences at their discretion, regardless of a licensee's previous record.

The Board Room, Carlisle, Cumbria. As a major munitions centre during the First World War the city came under the most draconian control in all Britain, with over fifty pubs suppressed and two breweries closed. The government feared that munitions workers on boom-time wages would jeopardise output unless drinking was severely restricted. By 1921 Carlisle had one pub to every 810 people, compared to the national average of 375.

19

APART FROM DRINKING

In Victorian working-class communities independent artisans segregated themselves from mere labourers. Skilled Bradford wool-combers avoided pubs used by lower members of their craft. Publicans maintained respectability by barring loafers, rowdies and criminals and setting limits to profanity and coarseness. Gambling on cards or dominoes or other games was common in rougher houses, despite the risk of fines or even loss of licence.

Entertainment, however, was good for business. The 'free-and-easy', a Saturday evening Regency version of karaoke, with customers providing their own songs and recitations, began to develop into 'music-hall' around 1840. The earliest music-halls were literally extensions of particularly enterprising pubs – both physically, as accommodations tacked on to existing premises, and organisationally, as shows managed by publicans, providing and co-ordinating amateur or professional talents. London led, most famously with the celebrated Grecian Saloon attached to the Eagle in

Off-sales – an enterprising Ipswich publican takes advantage of a local race meeting to generate extra sales by organising a refreshment tent.

20

City Road, but the rapidly expanding industrial cities followed soon after. In 1848 John Balmbra established a music-hall at his pub in Newcastle's Cloth Market. In 1862 it premiered the Geordie anthem, 'The Blaydon Races'. By 1866 London had over twenty music-halls and the provinces some three hundred. By 1880 free-standing music-halls were major institutions in their own right but smaller pub-based ones also survived, both types upholding the tradition of raucous audience participation.

Some establishments provided attractions in the tradition of eighteenth-century pleasure-grounds such as Vauxhall and Ranelagh – balloon ascents and firework displays at the Eyre Arms Tavern at St John's Wood, outdoor dancing at the Highbury Barn Tavern, cricket and pigeon-shooting at the Rosemary Branch in Peckham. In the 1880s there were still pubs putting on boxing matches, running or rowing races, offering the chance to place bets on the participants. Less-favoured establishments offered coarser, illegal distractions such as dog-fights, cock-fights and ratting.

It was in the then Wheatsheaf public house, Newcastle upon Tyne, in 1862 that the entertainer George Ridley first performed 'The Blaydon Races', which became the Geordie anthem. The pub was rebuilt in 1902 and latterly known as 'Balmbra's' after a former landlord, John Balmbra.

MEETINGS AND CLUBS

The pub was an informal working-men's club, not the mere retailer of oblivion caricatured by disapproving middle-class do-gooders. Regular clients used it for business as well as socialising. There were few alternatives. Reading rooms were under middle-class control, school premises operated under a religious regime. Neither favoured political or trade-union activities. Trade-union subscriptions and benefits were paid on licensed premises. Officials and members met in private upstairs rooms, supplied free on the understanding that participants would spend freely on drink. Likewise Freemasons and friendly societies, the latter in 1872 having four million members, compared with 500,000 trade unionists.

Pubs also organised savings clubs for clothing or boots or the financing of an annual expedition to a race meeting, the country or seaside, and they often provided support in a crisis, when a 'whip round' could raise funds for a 'regular' distressed by illness or accident or to pay for funeral expenses. Publicans often doubled as unofficial pawnbrokers and moneylenders.

Tramping artisans relied on pubs as 'houses of call' for information on local jobs. They were issued by their union with a 'blank' or 'clearance', entitling the bearer to supper, lodging and, if work was unavailable, a further allowance to carry them on. Initial support would come from their own union branch; after that it was up to each local branch to give the visitor enough to get him on to the next branch, but arrangements may well have varied between trades. Tramping, practised by the craft specialists in the printing, clothing, building and engineering trades, declined by the 1880s, although compositors and stonemasons carried on into the twentieth century.

Dog-fanciers and pigeon racers used pubs as the headquarters of their clubs.

The Knights of St John's Tavern hosted the inaugural dinner at which the St John's Wood Arts Club was formed. As an after-dinner entertainment the distinguished painter Sir Lawrence Alma-Tadema had his silhouette drawn on the wall. The unappreciative licensee had it whitewashed over and the club chose the Eyre Arms Tavern instead as its first clubhouse.

A handsome wall plaque on the Leopard in Burton upon Trent, Staffordshire, proclaims it as a meeting place of the United Order of Smiths (established 1822) – motto 'Industry and Benevolence United Us in Friendship'. Notice the precision lathe and beam engine to the left and the figure of a tramping artisan at lower right.

Other groups and events based in pubs included bands, choirs, flower shows, allotment societies, angling clubs and teams for bowling, quoits, darts, cycling, dog racing and clog dancing. Where such activities could involve a competitive element, pub competed against pub. In 1885 pubs in the mining communities of south Northumberland provided facilities for 39 per cent of recorded competitions.

NAMES AND SIGNS

Licensed premises continued to display signs after street numbering became general from the 1770s onwards. In culturally conservative Britain, ancient icons, namely the monarchy, retained symbolic power. Victoria, Albert and their prolific line were naturally lionised. Of British heroes Lord Nelson and the Duke of Wellington ranked supreme, of foreigners Garibaldi. The Crimean conflict and imperial engagements inspired dedications to remote battles and whiskery heroes such as Raglan, Napier, Havelock and Gordon. Victorian technology made less cultural impact on contemporaries than on posterity, though pubs were named for the Crystal Palace and its designer, Joseph Paxton. Far more pervasive was the transport revolution, inspiring hundreds of Railway Arms, Hotels, Inns and Taverns. The Victorian occupational structure was reflected, though very

Above: *First built in 1845 in consequence of the laying out of Victoria Street, Westminster, and originally named the Blue Coat Boy after an adjacent charity school, the Albert was rebuilt in 1865–7 and renamed after the recently deceased Prince Consort. Much favoured by Members of Parliament, as well as by tourists, it has a division bell to give tippling legislators an eight-minute warning of an imminent vote.*

The Crimean War of 1854–6 was the only major European conflict involving the Victorian army and was the first to be covered by professional journalists, thus magnifying its impact on the popular imagination. This sign in Harwich, Essex, commemorates a preliminary engagement of 20th September 1854 along the line of the river Alma at which the Russians failed to block an Anglo-French advance on their main stronghold, Sebastopol, thanks to the resolution of the British infantry.

'Punch' magazine traced its origins to a group of journalists who frequented the parlour of the Edinburgh Castle in the Strand, London, in 1841; when the magazine's staff subsequently gave their regular patronage to the Crown and Sugar Loaf in Fleet Street, it changed its name to the Punch Tavern.

partially, in pub names punning on 'Arms'. The building trades were most prominently represented by 'Arms' named for Bricklayers, Builders, Carpenters, Joiners, Masons, Painters and Plasterers. Other commonly represented occupations included Brewers, Coopers, Gardeners, Shipwrights and Watermen.

As the century progressed the traditional painted hanging sign, especially in urban areas, was increasingly abandoned in favour of an inscribed name-panel or entablature integral to the architecture of the building. By the 1880s, as big brewers strengthened their hold on the trade, and basic literacy became all but universal, the emphasis was increasingly in favour of bold lettering advertising the proprietorial brewery and its products rather than the pub itself.

Left: *Local hero – the John Snow in Broadwick Street, Soho, London, commemorates the locally resident doctor (and royal obstetrician) who proved in a triumph of medical detection that cholera is a water-borne disease. The pub stands opposite the site of the pump he identified as the source of the 1848–9 epidemic. Snow might have felt ambiguous about the compliment – he was a teetotaller.*

Below: *The Bottle and Glass Inn, reconstructed at the Black Country Museum in Dudley, West Midlands, eschews a painted sign in favour of simple lettering. Differing little from a modest but respectable mid-century domestic dwelling, its only architectural extravagance is a pair of bow windows.*

BEHIND THE BAR

The two names of this celebrated pub in London's East End encapsulate a living tradition. Allegedly the sailor son of the widowed owner would return home at Easter each year for her home-baked buns. When he failed one year to do so she continued to bake and save them. Each year a sailor adds one more to the basket of fossilised buns hanging above the bar. The pub dates back to at least 1810 but was rebuilt about half a century later.

Publicans came from many walks of life: some were the children of publicans who had grown up in the trade; others had backgrounds in related commercial professions, such as the shopkeeper or travelling salesman; there was the speculative builder investing a nest egg; or the former domestic servant, bringing system and discipline to the management of a house; ex-servicemen and former policemen also adopted the trade, bringing a firm hand to keeping order – providing they did not themselves fall prey to drink (in 1890–2 the death rate from alcoholism for London publicans was nine times the average for employed males). Minor music-hall or circus stars traded on fading celebrity. Former sportsmen, especially jockeys and boxers, traditionally gravitated to the licensed trade, although not always to flourish financially. Prominent examples included Tom Cribb, his rival James Belcher, and Belcher's younger brother Tom, whose pub was taken by Cribb's friend Tom Spring, promoter of a famous – illegal – boxing contest between publican Benjamin Caunt and William 'Bendigo' Thompson, the latter of whom eventually took the pledge and became a preacher. Middleweight champion James 'Jem' Mace combined boxing with being a publican and a circus performer – he fought in North America and Australia, keeping a pub in Melbourne. Sandhurst riding instructor Sergeant Major Alfred Savigear retired at the age of thirty-nine to run the Prince of Teck in Earl's Court Road, London. He also built shops and flats in nearby Kenway Road, developed London's largest covered riding school, rebuilt the Railway Hotel at Acton, ran the Swiss Cottage, owned a fleet of taxis and helped initiate the Royal Tournament.

A glass 'snob screen', inserted to preserve social distance between bar staff and drinkers.

Publicans with such substantial independent resources were, however, untypical. As tenants, many in London and in some provincial cities, such as Leeds, were heavily indebted to a brewery for their mortgage. In Liverpool, Manchester and Birmingham, by contrast, brewery policy was to install managers rather than tenants.

Barmen, invariably unmarried, lived in, averaging wages of up to a pound a week for 80–88 hours, less laundry charges for shirts and aprons. Barmaids often worked shifts and shorter hours, benefiting from tips in the better bars. Potmen, general dogsbodies, lived out and touted for extra pennies as billiard-markers (who kept score during a game). From *c.*1880 tills and monthly stocktakings greatly reduced staff opportunities for pilfering.

DRINK AND DISTRESS

Beer! Happy produce of our isle,
Can sinewy strength impart,
And wearied with fatigue and toil,
Can cheer each manly heart.

Despite the falling price of tea and coffee, the heavy drinking of alcohol remained integral to working-class life. In Scotland and Ireland this included spirits, in England and Wales mainly beer. Porter gave way to the thinner 'mild', often known as 'four-ale' because it sold at 4d a quart, hence 'four-ale bar' for the public bar. Saloon-bar patrons might prefer bitter at 3d or even 4d per pint. Irish whiskey challenged gin from the 1860s, both being overtaken by Scotch by the 1880s. Gin remained popular with women, as did port. Rum, priced the same, was favoured by seagoing types of the world's largest navy, merchant marine and fishing fleet. Brandy, at twice the price of other spirits, was for toffs.

Drink, regarded as 'manly' and 'strengthening', was a normal accompaniment to meals and was credited with 'putting the sweat back', keeping out the cold, sharpening appetite, inducing sleep and keeping bowels regular. Drink expressed the sociability appropriate to marking apprenticeships begun or ended, betrothals, marriage, promotion, removal to other employment, funerals and holiday wakes. A man who would not drink was odd, uncongenial and at risk of jeopardising his employment. In the 1830s a third of London's factory employees still kept 'St Monday', prolonging weekend drinking to return to work with a thick head on Tuesday. In the Potteries some slaved from Wednesday to Saturday to finance a regular three-day weekend binge. Higher-paid craftsmen in the provinces continued to drink out Mondays until well past mid-century and the advent of regularised holidays.

Professor Geoffrey Best has argued that 'it was statistically demonstrable that the deeper the poverty, the denser the pubs'. In Oxford, where gentlemanly undergraduates did most of their drinking in college, the greatest concentration of licensed

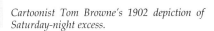

Cartoonist Tom Browne's 1902 depiction of Saturday-night excess.

28

The Maritime Inn of 1844 in the Barbican, Plymouth, Devon, was one of many pubs in the area popular with crews from the naval and fishing fleets.

premises was in industrial Jericho and slummy St Ebbe's and St Clement's. Leafy 'North Oxford' had only four licensed premises; Jericho, less than a fifth of the size, had twenty-nine. Ports also had heavy concentrations of pubs, where sailors and fishermen, after weeks at sea, were eager to spend.

" A TOLERABLY BROAD HINT "

Cabby (after driving a couple of miles, suddenly stops opposite a roadside Public House).
" Oh, I beg your pardon, Sir, but you didn't say as we was to pull up anywheres, did you, Sir ? "

This 'Punch' cartoon by J. Leech appeared in 1859.

The whimsical Blackfriar opposite Blackfriars station in London commemorates a medieval Dominican friary. A very rare example of licensed premises in the Arts and Crafts style, it has been described by Harwood and Saint as 'a genuine working City pub still, not an aesthetic tourist trap'. Originally built in 1875, it was given a make-over by H. Fuller Clark in 1904–6, the sculptures being the work of Frederick Callcott. The spectacularly marble-lined back bar known as 'The Grotto', featuring panels by Royal Academician Henry Poole, was a much later addition of 1917–21.

THE GREAT BUILDING BOOM

The profusion of drinking places made advertising superfluous. In 1848 the local coroner claimed Bolton had enough drinking places physically to accommodate the entire population – one for every twenty-five houses; in 1869 the town's licensed premises peaked at 452, for 80,000 inhabitants.

Slum missionary J. M. Weylland noted 'a sudden enlargement of public-houses and in the attractiveness of them' in the 1860s. John Ruskin, in newly suburbanised Camberwell, deplored the fact that 'scarcely a public house near the Crystal Palace but sells its gin and bitters under pseudo-Venetian capitals'. Pub building, extension and refurbishment was fuelled by a sustained rise in working-class purchasing power and the proliferation of alternative outlets for it. Cultivation of the prairies, pampas and outback in the decade 1877–87 slashed a typical workman's food costs by 30 per cent. Brewers knew they were competing with the music-hall, professional football clubs,

The 1902 Beehive Hotel on Bigg Market, Newcastle upon Tyne, features elaborate tilework, festooned with extravagant ceramic detailing.

Above: *A faded legend on the façade of the Green Dragon Hotel, Hertford, claims it to have been in existence by 1621 and in 1903 it was rebuilt in a pseudo-Jacobean mode to match this date. Striking terracotta panels on its outbuildings reflect the variety of transport used by patrons. As mechanical breakdowns were routine a motor pit was a highly desirable facility.*

Left: *The Old Cock Tavern in Fleet Street, London, still boasted of its Tudor origins in 2003 – but was reincarnated in this architectural pastiche opposite its original location in the late nineteenth century.*

polytechnic evening classes, libraries, museums, galleries, swimming baths and parks. Ever-larger unions and friendly societies abandoned pubs for their own purpose-built premises. Breweries responded with new attractions such as billiard tables, mechanical musical boxes and automata. Darts, quoits, skittles and bowls needed no great expenditure but were convivial rather than solitary pastimes. New bar configurations enabled more drink to be

Not all rebuilding was on an heroic scale. The Jolly Sailor, at St Albans, Hertfordshire, dating back to 1827, was rebuilt in 1899.

31

The Queen's Head, Eastville, Bristol, presents a lavish polychrome brick façade to converging major routes but the rear of the building is of traditional stone construction.

served faster to more people. The space behind the counter was cut back. Ground-floor kitchens were moved to basements or upstairs, gardens and yards built over.

Between the 1870s and 1890s Liberals, drawing support from Nonconformist Wales and Scotland, allied themselves to the temperance lobby, while Tories became partisans of the 'beerage'.

Market pressures were released by a Tory election victory in 1895. In a six-year period the modest Cannon brewery of St John's Street, Clerkenwell, spent £250,000 on rebuilding pubs and £1,363,010 on buying 125 more. Burton-based Allsopp's spent £3,230,000 between 1896 and 1900 on acquisitions. The boom peaked in 1896–9 with what architectural historians Elain Harwood and Andrew Saint have called a vigour that 'beggars belief. It was the brewers' architectural revenge for the gradual closing down of one little hostelry after another by Victorian reformers and health fanatics.' In 1896 London, with 393 persons per pub, had a lower density than Leeds (345), Liverpool (279), Birmingham (215), Sheffield (176) or Manchester (168). But mere numbers were misleading. Size also mattered. Closure of insignificant beerhouses under temperance pressure was offset by new brewery-backed mega-pubs.

Extravagant faience tile decoration and a mosaic floor adorn the entrance of the Warrington Hotel, Maida Vale, London. Such decor not only struck a flamboyant note but was hard-wearing and easy to keep clean.

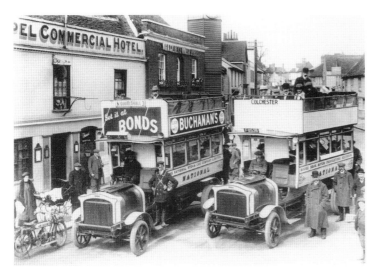

Like many ancient village hostelries, the Chapel Inn at Coggeshall, Essex, was refronted in the nineteenth century. From the early twentieth century it served as a departure point for early motor-bus services.

THE COUNTRY PUB

Rural survivors of the collapse of coaching at least benefited from a relatively wholesome image. In cities the church and the pub were oppositional but in villages they remained complementary. Some isolated premises were sustained by the willingness of the Victorians to combine epic walks with botanising, angling or a picnic. Annual influxes of harvesters brought seasonal boosts to income. Rural publicans often had by-employments. The 1851 census recorded 22,082 farmers, of whom 1,536 were also innkeepers and 1,898 beer-shop keepers. Other publicans worked in building or blacksmithing, ran a shop or post office, doubled as a miller or kept a 'dame school'. Rural pubs enjoyed a renaissance from the 1880s as the safety bicycle and motor car began to revive road traffic. Others were embraced by urban expansion, which brought them a new residential clientele.

The belated arrival of the railway in Fairford, Gloucestershire, in 1873 prompted the addition of this neo-classical extension to a clearly much older building, which was restyled 'The Railway Inn'. Tourist visitors to this handsome Cotswold town now provide a new source of custom.

TEMPERANCE

In 1829 an anti-spirit society was founded in Belfast, followed by others in Leeds and Bradford in 1830. In 1831 came the inaugural meeting of the London Temperance Society, later the British and Foreign Temperance Society.

In 1834, the very year in which the word 'teetotal' was coined (by Preston working man Richard Turner in the course of a speech advocating complete abstention from alcohol rather than mere abstinence from spirits), a Select Committee of the House of Commons investigated 'the prevailing Vice of Drunkenness' and called for more libraries, reading rooms, museums and parks as alternatives to pubs. Many of its regulatory recommendations were incorporated into the 1839 Act that inaugurated the assault on the worst excesses of the licensed trade.

In 1844 Thomas Cook organised the first ever railway excursion, between Leicester and Loughborough, to enable hundreds to hear a temperance campaigner. This advertisement for an excursion from Scarborough to Hull in 1872 reveals that temperance and train rides remained associated.

CHEAP TRIP TO HULL

ON EASTER TUESDAY, APRIL 2nd, 1872.

THE COMMITTEE OF THE SCARBOROUGH

WORKING MEN'S TEMPERANCE SOCIETY

Respectfully announce that they have arranged with the North Eastern Railway Company to run a Grand

EXCURSION TRAIN

TO THE POPULOUS TOWN OF

HULL

FROM

Scarborough, Filey, & Burlington,

ON EASTER TUESDAY, APRIL 2nd, 1872.

Recreation is necessary to the comfort and happiness of the people. Temperance Societies seek to promote healthy amusements as well as sobriety; and surely there cannot be a more agreeable mode of spending the Holidays---at Easter especially---than having an Excursion to some neighbouring town for a short relaxation from the cares and anxieties of business.

Pleasure Parties will be amply repaid, for there is something attractive at almost every turn. A ramble round the spacious Docks, Wharfs, Quays, and Steamboat Jetties, is worth a visit; these are probably the largest in the Kingdom. In the Market Place, near the South End, stands the noble equestrian gilded Statue of William III, erected in 1735. At the entrance of Junction Street is an elegant Doric Column, upwards of 72 feet in height, erected at a cost of £1,250, and known as the Wilberforce Monument, being a tribute to that great statesman and philanthropist, who was a native of Hull, and whose Statue surmounts the pillar. The Public Buildings in the town are numerous and elegant, to describe which would occupy considerably more space than the limits of this bill will allow.

Leave SCARBRO' at 7 a.m.; FILEY at 7-20 a.m.; BURLINGTON at 8 a.m.

FARES TO HULL AND BACK (COVERED CARRIAGES):

Scarborough and Filey, 2s. 6d.; Burlington, 1s. 6d.

CHILDREN UNDER TWELVE YEARS OF AGE, HALF-PRICE

THE TRAIN WILL RETURN FROM HULL AT 5 P.M.   NO LUGGAGE ALLOWED.

To prevent confusion and facilitate the departure of the train the Booking Offices at Scarborough, Filey, and Bridlington Railway Stations will be open on Saturday, March 30th, from 6-30 to 8 p.m., for the sale of Tickets; and on the morning of April 2nd, previous to departure of the train.

W. W. COOPLAND, PRINTER, SCARBORO'.

George Cruikshank, himself a toper turned teetotaller, provided graphic depictions of the alleged impact of alcohol on family life. His eight-part series 'The Bottle' sold 100,000 copies.

Temperance campaigners turned from urging moderation to demanding total abstention, finding a powerful spokesman in a former toper turned teetotaller, the artist George Cruikshank. Melodrama, pamphlets, slide lectures and school textbooks were all enlisted to a cause that blamed drink for poverty, crime, vice and dementia. Aristocratic landlords including the Dukes of Bedford and Westminster permitted only peripheral outlets for alcohol, as did model estates built by philanthropic employers in the provinces, such as Bessbrook, Bournville, Saltaire and Port Sunlight.

As *per capita* beer consumption rose to new heights, attempts were made to offer alternatives to the pub. In 1867 a British Workman's Public House was opened in Leeds, birthplace of the Band of Hope temperance campaign – to provide coffee, tea, cordials, snacks and papers in a pub-like setting. This formula was taken up in London

A London cabmen's shelter. Intended to provide a hot drink and meal day or night so that cabbies could stay out of pubs, the first of over sixty shelters opened in St John's Wood in 1875, though only about a dozen remained in 2003. Stars of theatre and music-hall, who relied on cabs to flit from one venue to the next and then take them home in the early hours, gladly supported cabmen's shelters with fund-raising performances.

Above left: *The founder of the Salvation Army, William Booth (1829–1912), began his preaching career outside pubs in Whitechapel, London, where his statue now stands. Booth blamed drink for diverting otherwise adequate incomes to waste, for domestic violence and for workplace injuries, which could deprive a family of its breadwinner.*

Above right: *Addressing the 1870 Annual General Meeting of the United Kingdom Alliance, Sir Wilfred Lawson MP (whose statue stands in the Embankment Gardens, London) suggested that the best thing that Britain could do was ship every publican off to the colonies. A lifelong campaigner against alcohol, he did succeed in outlawing the practice of paying agricultural labourers' wages partly in cider.*

by Dr Barnardo and Lord Shaftesbury, who converted a notorious Limehouse gin palace, the Edinburgh Castle, in 1873 and the Dublin Castle, Mile End Road, in 1875–6. In 1874 Shaftesbury's People's Cafe Company began to promote 'coffee-taverns' and in 1877 the Coffee Public House Association was established by the Duke of Westminster. By 1884 over 1500 coffee-houses had been established throughout the British Isles, 121 of them in London. Common facilities included a reading room and club room, billiard or bagatelle tables, organised concerts and discussion groups. Pubs still outnumbered them by over fifty to one.

If not the pub – then what? Small communities often failed to offer any alternative evening venue to the temptations of licensed premises. This former Temperance Hall in Hesket Newmarket, Cumbria, is now a private dwelling.

Both the Empire and the adjacent King's Arms in Barrow-in-Furness, Cumbria, have replaced their original ground-floor windows with sheet glass.

ENVOI

In 1890 there were nineteen pubs along Oxford Street, London; in 2003 only the Tottenham remained. Also in 1890 there were thirty pubs on the Strand, London, plus bars in hotels and restaurants; in 2003 they were outnumbered by coffee bars. The 1904 Licensing Act provided compensation for a pub closure from a levy on the licensed trade. Between 1906 and 1914 3736 pubs were closed, a crackdown

Hanging on – the Bushel Inn, Newmarket, Suffolk. A town devoted to racing is guaranteed to provide constant occasions for celebration and commiseration. The clothes and the poster referring to a radio supplement suggest a date c.1930.

The former Seven Stars, a classic late-Victorian corner-site pub on Bromley-by-Bow High Street, London, was converted to apartments in the 1980s. Three pubs – two of them Victorian – still remain in the quarter-mile street.

reinforced by rising unemployment, falling real wages, industrial unrest and mass emigration.

Surviving Victorian pubs have almost always undergone major internal changes. Façades survive in far greater numbers than do interiors. As Elain Harwood and Andrew Saint have cogently observed, 'where drinking takes place, nothing ornamental lasts very long'. Pubs have, however, benefited from growing conservationist sentiment since the mid twentieth century. Period features are now more likely to be preserved than in the 'Formica-fuelled Fifties'. But as Mark Girouard warned decades ago, 'the breweries are ... less prone to destruction than they were ... but they are continually altering, "improving", rearranging, renaming and touching up their Victorian pubs, sometimes with skill and tact but all too often with neither'.

FURTHER READING

Barr, A. *Drink: An Informal Social History*. Bantam, 1995.

Burke, T. *English Inns*. Collins, 1943.

Clarke, P. *The English Alehouse*. Longman, 1983.

Elwall, P. *Bricks and Beer: English Pub Architecture 1830–1939*. British Architectural Library, 1983.

Girouard, M. *Victorian Pubs*. Studio Vista/Yale University Press, 1975.

Harrison, B. *Drink and the Victorians*. Faber, 1971.

Harrison, B. 'Pubs' in *The Victorian City* (volume 1), edited by Dyos and Wolff. Routledge & Kegan Paul, 1973.

Harwood, E., and Saint, A. *London: Exploring England's Heritage*. HMSO, 1991.

Haydon, P. *The English Pub: A History*. Robert Hale, 1994.

Haydon, P. *Beer and Britannia: An Inebriated History of Britain*. Sutton Publishing, 2001.

Lamb, C. *Inn Signs*. Shire, 1976; reprinted 1987.

Lemmen, H. van. *Victorian Tiles*. Shire, second edition 2000.

Longmate, N. *The Waterdrinkers*. Hamish Hamilton, 1968.

Monckton, H.A. *A History of English Ale and Beer*. Bodley Head, 1966.

Monckton, H.A. *A History of the English Public House*. Bodley Head, 1969.

Osborn, H. *Inn and Around London: A History of Young's Pubs*. Young & Company's Brewery, 1991.

Pearson, L. F. *The Northumbrian Pub: An Architectural History*. Sandhill Press, 1989.

Spiller, B. *Victorian Public Houses*. David & Charles, 1972.

Wittich, J. *Discovering London's Inns and Taverns*. Shire, fourth edition 1996.

Transplanted – the Red Lion at Crich Tramway Village, Derbyshire, has been rebuilt from a dismantled pub in Hanley. Although the glass has been replaced, the ceramic decoration is original and has fortunately been retained. A similar exercise in reconstitution can be seen at Beamish, County Durham. The demolition of several traditional pubs in the North-east was accompanied by the swift exportation of their elaborate tilework to the United States by shrewd interior designers who acquired the fruits of fine craftsmanship at a knock-down price.

PLACES TO VISIT

The Bass Museum of Brewing Heritage, Horninglow Street, Burton upon Trent, Staffordshire DE14 1YQ. Telephone: 0845 600 0598. Website: www.bass-museum.com (A virtual tour of Burton in 1881 is accessible online.)

Beamish, The North of England Open Air Museum, Beamish, County Durham DH9 0RG. Telephone: 0191 370 4000. Website: www.beamish.org.uk (Has a reconstructed pub, the Sun Inn.)

Black Country Living Museum, Tipton Road, Dudley, West Midlands DY1 4SQ. Telephone: 0121 557 9643. Website: www.bclm.co.uk (Has a reconstructed pub, the Bottle and Glass Inn.)

Crich Tramway Village, near Matlock, Derbyshire DE4 5DP. Telephone: 01773 852565. Website: www.tramway.co.uk (Has the rebuilt Red Lion from Hanley, with original ceramic decoration.)

Luton Museum and Gallery, Wardown Park, Old Bedford Road, Luton LU2 7HA. Telephone: 01582 546722. Website: www.luton.gov.uk/enjoying/museums (Has the bar from the Plough, George Street, Luton, built 1833.)

Milestones, Hampshire's Living History Museum, Leisure Park, Churchill Way West, Basingstoke, Hampshire RG21 6YR. Telephone: 01256 477766. Website: www.milestones-museum.com (Includes a pub dispensing Gales' special Milestones ale.)

Museum of London, London Wall, London EC2Y 5HN. Telephone: 0870 444 3852. Website: www.museum-london.org.uk (Has a small reconstruction of a bar in its Victorian street.)

Salford Museum, Peel Park Crescent, Salford M5 4WU. Telephone: 0161 736 2649. Website: www.salfordmuseum.org (Includes Lark Hill Place with a reconstructed Victorian pub, the Blue Lion.)

The sign of the Valiant Soldier in Buckfastleigh, Devon, asserts it to be a 'Fully Licensed' house – i.e. not just a beer shop. When it closed in the 1960s after two centuries as a village inn, the interior of the Victorian-fronted premises remained untouched – an act of unintended conservation which has enabled it to re-open as a museum exemplar of a mid-twentieth-century lifestyle.

WEBSITES

A–Z of Victorian London Taverns, Inns and Public Houses: www.gendocs.demon.co.uk/pubs.html

Aidan's London Pub Crawls: www.alpc.co.uk

British Beer and Pub Association: www.beerandpub.com

Family and Community Historical Research Society Pub History: www.sfowler.force9.co.uk/page-12.htm

A useful introduction to local pub and brewery history sites: www.btinternet.com/~steven.williams1/pubpgintro.htm